italian
cooking

Chef
express

Published by:
TRIDENT PRESS INTERNATIONAL
801 12th Avenue South, Suite 400
Naples, Fl 34102 USA
Tel: + 1 239 649 7077
Email: tridentpress@worldnet.att.net
Websites: www.trident-international.com
            www.chefexpressinternational.com

Italian Cooking
© Trident Press International

Publisher
Simon St. John Bailey

Editor-in-chief
Isabel Toyos

Includes Index
ISBN 1582797684
UPC 6 15269 97684 5

2004 Edition
Printed in Colombia by Cargraphics S.A.

introduction

The flavors of Italy came into the spotlight of
international cuisine when the Mediterranean
diet was widespread. In fact, today practically
all cooks have included in their menus some
type of definitely Italian dish. Multicolor
vegetables, cheeses of unique character,
proverbial pasta, intensely fragrant herbs,

fresh fish and seafood, garlic and olive oil make up a passionate, natural cuisine that seduces gourmets worldwide.

The products

Cheeses like the Parmesan, mascarpone, ricotta and mozzarella have already acquired international status. The prosciutto from Parma has a well earned reputation as an exquisitely refined ham. Herbs like basil, thyme, rosemary, sage, oregano are definitely meridional. And the simple Caprese salad (tomato, basil, mozzarella and olive oil) has become a typical delight anyone can enjoy. This cuisine that has crossed boundaries has even been known to create emblematic dishes with products originated in the Americas such as peppers and tomato.

The antipasto

Indispensable as the starter of a meal, it is the heart of the Italian table: an appetizer that combines vegetables, fish and seafood, cheese and cold cuts, plus a variety of olives and pickles that are never missing.

Pasta

A tradition that is present in all its forms: asciutta (dried) or fresh, filled or simple, always accompanied by tasty sauces. Cooking time varies for dried or fresh pasta, but all types need to be boiled in abundant salty water.

The desserts

Ice creams and cassatas prevail (remember the ancient Romans were the first to taste ice cream made from the snow obtained in the high mountains). The mascarpone –a creamy, dense, spread cheese–, along with coffee, is the basic ingredient for the celebrated tiramisu. At table talk biscotti are kings, the double baking giving them a more crunchy texture, enhanced by the nuts.

Difficulty scale

■□□ I Easy to do

■■□ I Requires attention

■■■ I Requires experience

tomato
and basil bruschetta

■□□ I Cooking time: 10 minutes - Preparation time: 15 minutes

ingredients
> ½ cup/125 ml/4 fl oz olive oil
> 2 cloves garlic, crushed
> 1 French bread stick, sliced diagonally
> 3 tomatoes, finely chopped
> 3 tablespoons chopped fresh basil or parsley
> freshly ground black pepper

method
1. Combine oil and garlic. Brush bread slices liberally with oil mixture and place on an oiled baking tray. Bake at 200°C/400°F/ Gas 6 for 10 minutes or until bread is golden. Set aside to cool.
2. Place tomatoes, basil or parsley and black pepper to taste in a bowl and mix to combine. Just prior to serving, top toasted bread slices with tomato mixture.

Serves 6

tip from the chef
For a light meal, top bruschetta with a little grated Parmesan or mozzarella cheese and grill until cheese melts. Serve with salad.

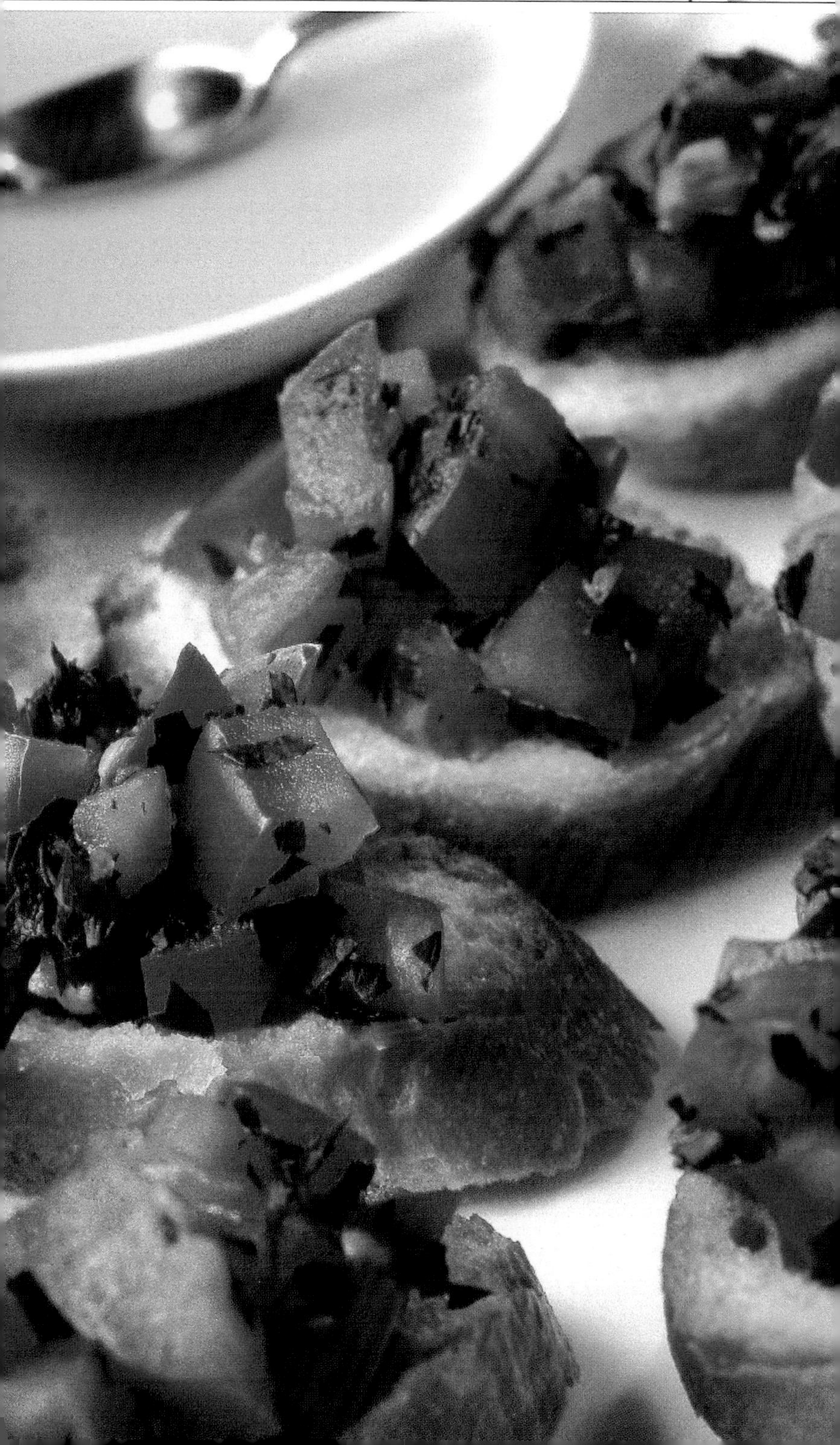

fresh
basil carpaccio

■□□ I Cooking time: 0 minutes - Preparation time: 25 minutes

method

1. To make dressing, place basil, oil, lemon juice, capers and garlic in a bowl. Mix well to combine.
2. Arrange beef slices on a serving plate and season with black pepper. Pour dressing over and sprinkle with onion. Cover and marinate for 10 minutes before serving.

....
Serves 4

ingredients

> **500 g/1 lb eye fillet, very thinly sliced**
> **1 onion, finely sliced**
> **freshly ground black pepper**

dressing

> **10 fresh basil leaves, chopped**
> **4 tablespoons olive oil**
> **3 tablespoons lemon juice**
> **2 tablespoons capers, chopped**
> **2 clove garlics, finely chopped**

tip from the chef

Carpaccio can be made with different types of meat, but it must always be carefully and very thinly sliced, almost transparent. To do so, the meat should be almost frozen at the moment of cutting.

sausage and roast peppers salad

■■■ | Cooking time: 15 minutes - Preparation time: 90 minutes

ingredients

> 125 g/4 oz penne, cooked and cooled
> 2 red peppers, roasted and cut into strips
> 2 yellow or green peppers, roasted and cut into strips
> 125 g/4 oz button mushrooms, sliced
> 155 g/5 oz pitted black olives
> 5 English spinach leaves, stalks removed and leaves finely chopped

herbed beef sausages

> 500 g/1 lb lean beef mince
> 185 g/6 oz sausage meat
> 2 cloves garlic, crushed
> 1 teaspoon chopped fresh rosemary
> 1 tablespoon finely chopped fresh basil
> 2 slices prosciutto or lean ham, finely chopped
> 1 tablespoon olive oil
> freshly ground black pepper

herb dressing

> $^1/_2$ cup/125 ml/4 fl oz olive oil
> $^1/_4$ cup/60 ml/2 fl oz balsamic or red wine vinegar
> 2 teaspoons chopped fresh basil or 1 teaspoon dried basil
> 1 teaspoon chopped fresh oregano or $^1/_4$ teaspoon dried oregano
> freshly ground black pepper

method

1. To make sausages, place beef, sausage meat, garlic, rosemary, basil, prosciutto or ham, olive oil and black pepper to taste in a bowl and mix to combine. Shape mixture into 10 cm/4 in long sausages. Cook sausages under a preheated medium grill, turning occasionally, for 10-15 minutes or until brown and cooked through. Set aside to cool slightly, then cut each sausage into diagonal slices.
2. To make dressing, place olive oil, vinegar, basil, oregano and black pepper to taste in a screwtop jar and shake well to combine.
3. Place sausage slices, penne, red and yellow or green peppers, mushrooms and olives in bowl, spoon over dressing and toss to combine. Line a serving platter with spinach leaves, then top with sausage and vegetable mixture.

....
Serves 4

tip from the chef

To prevent pasta for a salad from sticking together, rinse it under cold running water, immediately after draining. All this mouthwatering salad needs to make a complete meal is some crusty bread or wholemeal rolls.

leek
and basil frittata

■□□ | Cooking time: 18 minutes - Preparation time: 10 minutes

method

1. Place eggs, milk, Parmesan cheese and black pepper to taste in a bowl and whisk to combine. Set aside.
2. Heat oil in a 23 cm/9 in nonstick frying pan over a medium heat, add leeks and cook, stirring occasionally, for 8 minutes or until soft and golden.
3. Stir in eggplant and basil and cook for 1 minute. Pour egg mixture over vegetables and cook over a low heat for 7 minutes or until frittata is almost set. Place frittata under a preheated hot grill and cook for 1 minute or until top is golden and firm. Serve hot, warm or cold cut into wedges.

ingredients

> **5 eggs**
> **1/2 cup/125 ml/4 fl oz milk**
> **4 tablespoons grated Parmesan cheese**
> **freshly ground black pepper**
> **1 tablespoon olive oil**
> **2 leeks, chopped**
> **125 g/4 oz marinated char-grilled eggplant, cut into strips**
> **3 tablespoons fresh basil leaves**

....
Serves 4

tip from the chef

Char-grilled marinated eggplant is available from gourmet delicatessens. To make your own marinated eggplant, marinate char-grilled eggplant in olive oil and lemon juice, seasoned to taste with freshly ground black pepper, for at least 2 hours. For a spicy kick, add some finely chopped red chili.

hearty
macaroni soup

■■□ | Cooking time: 15 minutes - Preparation time: 40 minutes

ingredients

> **2 teaspoons vegetable oil**
> **1 red onion, chopped**
> **2 fresh red chilies, seeded and finely chopped**
> **1 red pepper, chopped**
> **2 carrots, chopped**
> **2 zucchini, sliced**
> **4 cups/1 liter/1³/4 pt vegetable stock**
> **440 g/14 oz canned tomatoes, undrained and mashed**
> **250 g/8 oz elbow macaroni**
> **440 g/14 oz canned red kidney beans, rinsed**
> **1 tablespoon finely chopped fresh thyme or ¹/2 teaspoon dried thyme**
> **freshly ground black pepper**

method

1. Heat oil in a large saucepan over a medium heat. Add onion and chilies and cook, stirring, for 3 minutes or until onion is soft.
2. Add red pepper, carrots, zucchini, stock, tomatoes and macaroni, bring to simmering and simmer for 10 minutes or until macaroni is cooked.
3. Stir in beans and thyme, bring to simmering and simmer for 2 minutes or until heated through. Season to taste with black pepper.

....
Serves 4

tip from the chef

This hearty pasta and vegetable soup makes a substantial one-dish meal. While the recipe uses macaroni you can in fact use any pasta you wish. Soups are a great way of using up any odds and ends of pasta you may have in the cupboard.

roasted
eggplant soup

■■□ I Cooking time: 21 minutes- Preparation time: 40 minutes

method

1. Place eggplant and red peppers, skin side up under a preheated hot grill (a) and cook for 10 minutes or until flesh is soft and skins are blackened. Peel away blackened skin and roughly chop flesh.

2. Heat oil in a large saucepan over a medium heat. Add garlic and tomatoes (b) and cook, stirring, for 2 minutes. Add eggplant, red peppers, stock (c) and black pepper, bring to simmer and leave for 4 minutes. Remove pan from heat and set aside to cool slightly.

3. Place vegetables and stock in batches in food processor or blender and process until smooth. Return mixture to a clean pan, bring to simmer over a medium heat and simmer for 3-5 minutes or until heated through.

ingredients

> 1 kg/2 lb eggplant, halved
> 4 red peppers, halved
> 1 teaspoon olive oil
> 2 cloves garlic, crushed
> 4 tomatoes, peeled and chopped
> 3 cups/750 ml/1¼ pt vegetable stock
> 2 teaspoons crushed black peppercorns

tip from the chef

This soup can be made the day before and reheated when required.

....
Serves 6

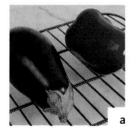

a   b   c

mixed
mushroom risotto

■■□ | Cooking time: 35 minutes - Preparation time: 30 minutes

method

1. In a pan, heat the butter, add the mushrooms, and cook for a few minutes. Remove from the heat and set aside.
2. Heat the oil in a large heavy-based saucepan, add the garlic and leek, and cook for 5-6 minutes until cooked. Meanwhile, place stock in a saucepan and simmer gently.
3. Add the rice and stir for 1 minute, coating the rice in oil. Add the white wine, and cook until liquid is absorbed. Start adding the stock a ladle at a time, stirring continuously until liquid has been absorbed. Continue adding stock a ladle at a time until stock is used and rice is cooked.
4. Stir in mushrooms, lemon rind, cheeses and parsley and serve immediately.

ingredients

> 2 tablespoons butter
> 500 g/1 lb mixed mushrooms (oyster, shiitake, flat, enoki, Swiss), sliced
> 40 ml/1 1/2 fl oz olive oil
> 2 cloves garlic, minced
> 1 leek, finely sliced
> 1 liter/1 3/4 pt chicken stock
> 2 cups arborio rice
> 1/2 cup/120 ml/4 fl oz white wine
> rind of 1 lemon, finely grated
> 1/2 cup/60 g/2 oz each pecorino and Parmesan cheese, grated
> 2 tablespoons parsley, chopped

....
Serves 6-8

tip from the chef

For the perfect risotto, stock should be added little by little while cooking. Italian arborio rice, of rounded grain and very white, is the most suitable for this dish.

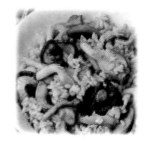

prosciutto
and fig pizzas

■□□ | Cooking time: 15 minutes - Preparation time: 10 minutes

ingredients

> **4 ready-made individual pizza bases**
> **2 teaspoons olive oil**
> **125 g/4 oz prosciutto**
> **4 fresh or dried figs, sliced**
> **60 g/2 oz pine nuts**
> **1 tablespoon chopped fresh rosemary or 1/2 teaspoon dried rosemary**
> **freshly ground black pepper**

method

1. Place pizza bases on lightly greased baking trays.
2. Brush bases with oil and top with prosciutto and fig slices. Sprinkle with pine nuts, rosemary and black pepper to taste.
3. Bake at 190°C/375°F/Gas 5 for 10-15 minutes or until bases are crisp and golden.

....
Serves 4

tip from the chef

Perfect for an autumn luncheon when fresh figs are in season and at their best. For a complete meal accompany with garlic bread, a salad and a glass of dry white wine.

pizza
supreme

■■□ | Cooking time: 15 minutes - Preparation time: 40 minutes

method

1. Place pizza bases on lightly greased baking trays and spread with tomato paste (purée).
2. Arrange half the green pepper, peperoni or salami, ham or prosciutto, mushrooms, pineapple and olives attractively on each pizza base.
3. Combine mozzarella cheese and tasty cheese (mature Cheddar) and sprinkle half the mixture over each pizza. Bake at 200°C/400°F/Gas 6 for 10-15 minutes or until cheese is golden and bases are crisp.

Serves 8

ingredients

> **2 ready-made pizza bases**
> **³/4 cup/185 ml/6 fl oz tomato paste (purée)**
> **1 green pepper, chopped**
> **155 g/5 oz sliced peperoni or salami**
> **155 g/5 oz ham or prosciutto, sliced**
> **125 g/4 oz mushrooms, sliced**
> **440 g/14 oz canned pineapple pieces, drained**
> **60 g/2 oz pitted olives**
> **125 g/4 oz mozzarella cheese, grated**
> **125 g/4 oz tasty cheese (mature Cheddar), grated**

tip from the chef

If you only want to make one pizza, halve the topping ingredients and use only one pizza base. But remember everyone loves pizza and they always eat more than you –or they– think they will.

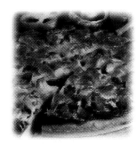

spaghetti
carbonara

■□□ I Cooking time: 15 minutes - Preparation time: 15 minutes

ingredients

> **185 g/6 oz slices ham, cut into strips**
> **4 eggs**
> **1/3 cup/90 ml/3 fl oz cream**
> **90 g/3 oz grated fresh Parmesan cheese**
> **500 g/1 lb spaghetti**
> **freshly ground black pepper**

method

1. Cook ham in a nonstick frying pan for 2-3 minutes. Place eggs, cream and Parmesan cheese in a bowl and beat lightly to combine.

2. Cook spaghetti in boiling water in a large saucepan following packet directions. Drain spaghetti, add egg mixture and ham and toss so that the heat of the spaghetti cooks the sauce. Season to taste with black pepper and serve immediately.

....
Serves 4

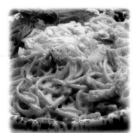

tip from the chef

Spaghetti, along with pizza and frittatas, form the basis of this cuisine. The pasta is then combined with the fish and seafood that abound in the peninsula.

penne with gorgonzola sauce

■□□ | Cooking time: 20 minutes - Preparation time: 15 minutes

method

1. Cook pasta in boiling water in a large saucepan following packet directions. Drain, set aside and keep warm.
2. To make sauce, place cream, stock, wine and Gorgonzola or blue cheese in a saucepan and cook, over a medium heat, stirring constantly, until smooth. Bring to simmering and simmer for 8 minutes or until sauce thickens.
3. Add parsley, nutmeg and black pepper to taste to sauce, bring to simmering and simmer for 2 minutes. Spoon sauce over hot pasta.

Serves 4

ingredients

> 500 g/1 lb penne

gorgonzola sauce

> 1 cup/250 ml/8 fl oz cream (double)
> 1/2 cup/125 ml/4 fl oz vegetable stock
> 1/2 cup/125 ml/4 fl oz white wine
> 125 g/4 oz Gorgonzola or blue cheese, crumbled
> 2 tablespoons chopped flat-leaf parsley
> 1/2 teaspoon ground nutmeg
> freshly ground black pepper

tip from the chef

Reheating pasta can be done successfully, if it is already combined with a sauce. To reheat, place in a greased ovenproof dish, cover with foil, and reheat in a moderate oven.

pasta with anchovies and basil sauce

■□□ | Cooking time: 20 minutes - Preparation time: 30 minutes

ingredients

> **250 ml/8 fl oz olive oil**
> **2 cloves garlic, crushed**
> **8 anchovy fillets, reserve oil**
> **2 punnets cherry tomatoes, halved**
> **20 fresh basil leaves, roughly chopped**
> **12 sun-dried tomatoes, sliced**
> **2 teaspoons capers**
> **500 g/1 lb egg fettuccine**
> **1/2 cup fresh basil, chopped**
> **freshly ground black pepper**

method

1. Heat the oil and sauté garlic and anchovies until garlic is just yellow in color. Turn heat to very low, then toss halved tomatoes, basil leaves, sun-dried tomatoes and capers in with the anchovies and oil.
2. Cook pasta in boiling, salted water until al dente and drain thoroughly. Pour sauce over fresh pasta and garnish with fresh chopped basil and sprinkle black pepper to taste.

....

Serves 4

tip from the chef

The basic dough for pasta is composed of 400 g/14 oz flour, 4 eggs, 1 tablespoon olive oil and salt. This formula will allow you to make all types of pasta.

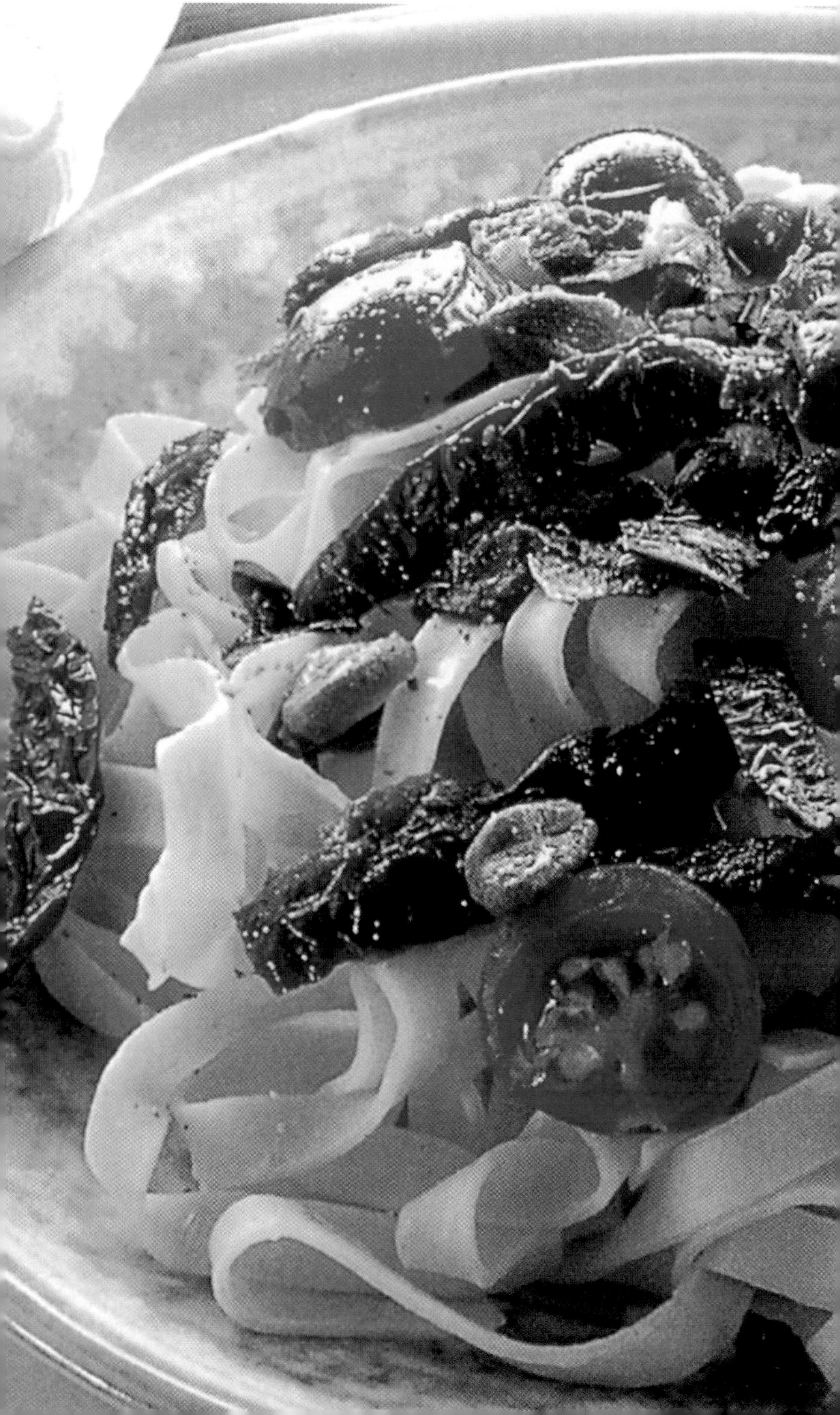

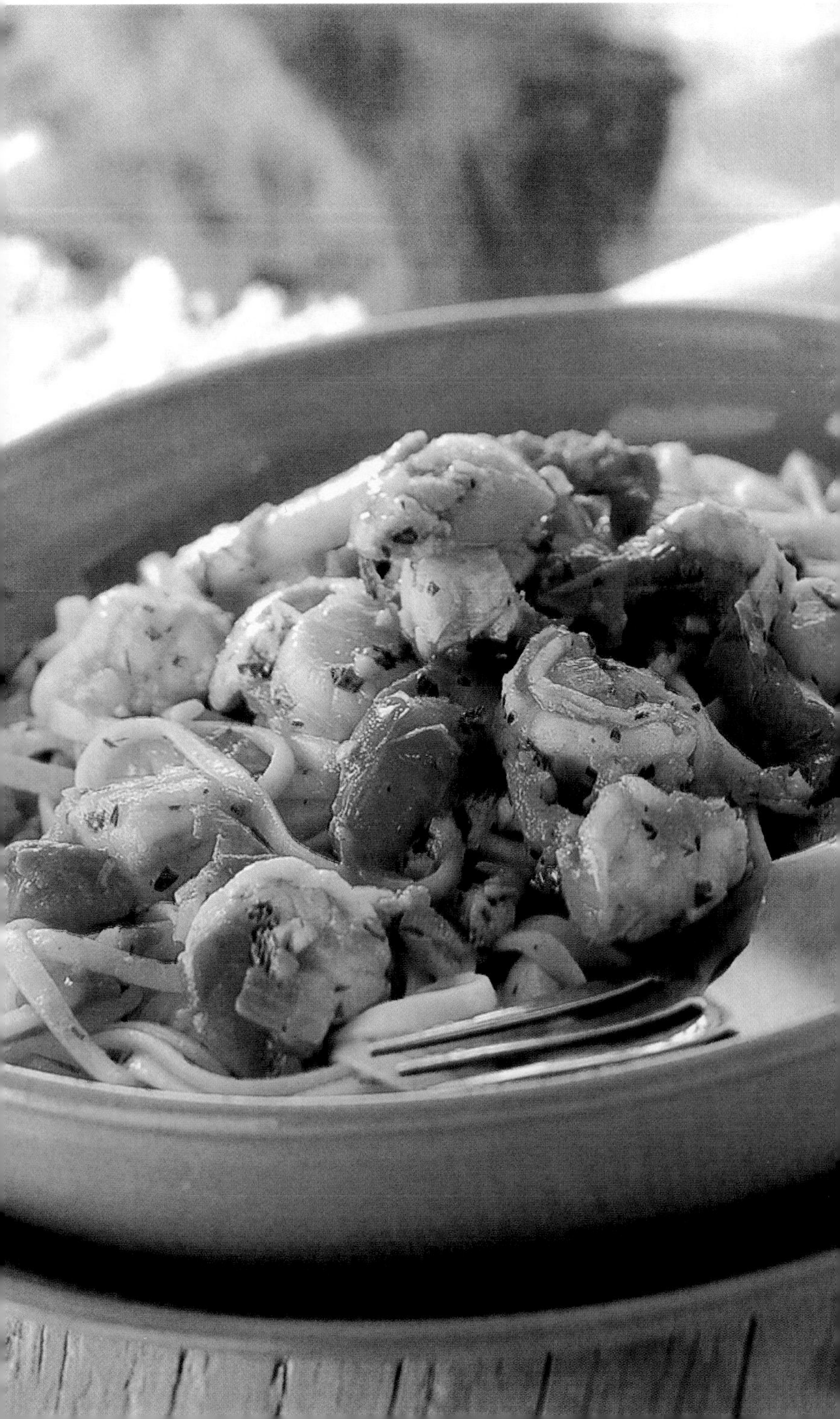

linguine with prawns and scallops

■ ■ ■ | Cooking time: 55 minutes - Preparation time: 50 minutes

method

1. Cook the linguine in salted boiling water until al dente and set aside.
2. Preheat oven at 180°C/350°F/Gas 4. Cut the tomatoes in half and place on a baking tray. Drizzle with a little olive oil, sprinkle with a little salt and pepper, and roast in the oven for 20-25 minutes until tomatoes are well roasted.
3. Place roasted tomatoes in a food processor and process for a few seconds, but do not over-process. (The mixture should still have texture.)
4. Heat half the oil in a pan. Sauté the scallops and the prawns for 2 minutes until just cooked, and remove from the pan. Add the calamari and cook for 2 minutes, before removing from the pan. Adding a little more oil if needed, sauté the fish for a few minutes until just cooked, and remove from the pan.
5. Heat the remaining oil, and sauté the garlic and onion for a few minutes until cooked. Add the tomato mixture, tomato paste and water, and simmer for 10 minutes. Carefully add the seafood to the sauce, season with salt and pepper, and mix through the chopped parsley.
6. Serve with the linguine and Parmesan cheese.

....
Serves 4

ingredients

> 400 g/13 oz linguine
> 1 kg/2 lb tomatoes
> salt and pepper
> 80 ml/3 fl oz olive oil
> 200 g/7 oz scallops
> 200 g/7 oz green prawns, peeled
> 150 g calamari, cut into rings
> 200 g/7 oz firm white fish pieces
> 3 cloves garlic, crushed
> 2 brown onions, diced
> 1 tablespoon tomato paste (optional)
> 80 ml/3 fl oz water
> 1/3 cup/20 g/2/3 oz parsley, chopped
> Parmesan cheese, grated

tip from the chef

Sauces with seafood go great with all pasta. For a simple and quick formula, stir-fry prawns and a clove of garlic (whole) in olive oil. Add drained pasta and garnish with a handful of finely chopped parsley.

spaghetti
with meatballs

■■□ | Cooking time: 50 minutes - Preparation time: 45 minutes

ingredients

> **500 g/1 lb lean minced beef**
> **2 tablespoons chopped fresh parsley**
> **60 g/2 oz salami, very finely chopped**
> **60 g/2 oz grated Parmesan cheese**
> **3 tablespoons tomato purée**
> **1 egg, beaten**
> **15 g/¹/₂ oz butter**
> **1 onion, very finely chopped**
> **2 teaspoons dried basil**
> **1 teaspoon dried oregano**
> **440 g/14 oz canned tomatoes, chopped**
> **125 ml/4 fl oz beef stock**
> **125 ml/4 fl oz white wine**
> **1 teaspoon caster sugar**
> **250 g/8 oz spaghetti**

method

1. Combine beef, parsley, salami, Parmesan cheese and 1 tablespoon tomato purée in a bowl (a), mix in enough egg to bind. Form mixture into small balls (b), cook in a nonstick frying pan (c) for 10-12 minutes until cooked, then set aside.

2. Melt butter in a large frying pan over moderate heat. Add onion, basil and oregano and cook for 2 minutes. Stir in tomatoes, remaining tomato purée, beef stock, wine and sugar. Simmer mixture for 30 minutes, stirring occasionally, until thick.

3. Cook spaghetti in boiling salted water until just tender, drain. Stir meatballs into the tomato sauce, warm through, stirring occasionally. Serve on a bed of spaghetti.

....

Serves 4

tip from the chef

To cut down on preparation time make the meatballs in advance and freeze them in the tomato sauce in a covered container for up to 3 months. Simply reheat over a gentle heat when required and serve with spaghetti.

a

b

c

spinach
and ricotta cannelloni

■■□ | Cooking time: 40 minutes - Preparation time: 45 minutes

method

1. To make filling, place spinach and water in a saucepan, cover with a tight fitting lid and cook over a medium heat, shaking pan occasionally, for 4-5 minutes or until spinach wilts. Drain well, squeezing out excess water and set aside to cool.

2. Finely chop spinach and place in a bowl. Add ricotta cheese, Parmesan cheese, egg, nutmeg and black pepper to taste and mix to combine. Spoon mixture into cannelloni tubes and arrange tubes side-by-side in a lightly greased ovenproof dish.

3. Combine tomatoes and garlic in a bowl and spoon over cannelloni. Sprinkle with mozzarella cheese and Parmesan cheese and bake at 180°C/350°F/Gas 4 for 30-35 minutes or until cannelloni is tender and top is golden.

....
Serves 4

ingredients

> 250 g/8 oz instant (no precooking required) cannelloni tubes
> 440 g/14 oz canned tomatoes, drained and chopped
> 1 clove garlic, crushed
> 125 g/4 oz grated mozzarella cheese
> 2 tablespoons grated Parmesan cheese

spinach filling

> 1/2 bunch/250 g/8 oz English spinach, shredded
> 1/2 cup/125 ml/4 fl oz water
> 250 g/8 oz ricotta cheese, drained
> 2 tablespoons grated Parmesan cheese
> 1 egg, beaten
> 1/4 teaspoon ground nutmeg
> freshly ground black pepper

tip from the chef

Cottage cheese may be used in place of the ricotta cheese if you wish. If using cottage cheese, push through a sieve to achieve a smoother texture. Serve cannelloni with an Italian salad and herb or garlic bread.

chicken
cannelloni

■■■ | Cooking time: 60 minutes - Preparation time: 45 minutes

ingredients

> **2 tablespoons olive oil or butter**
> **3/4 cup/90 g/3 oz flour**
> **1 onion, finely chopped**
> **4 cups/1 liter/13/4 pt milk**
> **500 g/1 lb ground chicken**
> **3 rashers bacon, chopped**
> **salt, pepper**
> **3 tablespoons grated Parmesan cheese**
> **1/8 teaspoon nutmeg**
> **2 eggs, beaten**
> cannelloni tubes
> **1 cup/250 ml/8 oz tomato pasta sauce**
> **160 g/5 oz butter**
> **1/2 cup/125 ml/4 fl oz water**

method

1. Heat butter in a large pan, add onion and sauté 2 minutes, add ground chicken and bacon and stir until browned and cooked. Remove from heat. Add Parmesan cheese, salt and pepper to taste. Set aside.

2. Make a bechamel sauce by melting the 160 g/5 oz butter in a saucepan, add flour and stir 1 minute. Remove from heat, gradually add milk, stirring well. Return to heat, stir until sauce thickens and boils. Remove from heat, stir in seasonings, cheese and eggs. Fill cannelloni tubes with chicken mixture.

3. Grease a large oven dish. Mix pasta sauce and water together and spread half over base of dish. Place cannelloni tubes in two rows in the dish then pour over remaining pasta sauce. Pour over the bechamel sauce, spread evenly and sprinkle with a little grated Parmesan cheese. Dot with 2 teaspoons butter and bake in preheated oven at 180°C/350°F/Gas 4 for 30-35 minutes until golden brown. Serve hot with a tossed salad.

....
Serves 6

tip from the chef
For variation, use ground fish instead of chicken and add to sauce 5 chopped anchovy fillets, 1 crushed clove garlic and 75g/2 1/2 oz pitted black olives.

pork-and-sage
filled ravioli

■ ■ ■ | Cooking time: 5 minutes - Preparation time: 60 minutes

method

1. To make filling, place ricotta cheese, bacon, pork, parsley, sage and Parmesan cheese in a bowl. Mix to combine and season to taste with nutmeg and black pepper. Cover and set aside while making dough.

2. To make dough, place all ingredients in a food processor and process for about 30 seconds. If the mixture is wet to the touch, mix in flour by the tablespoon until the dough feels soft but not sticky; if the mixture is too dry to work with, blend in water by the tablespoon until the dough just forms a ball. Knead and roll out dough to 1 mm thick.

3. Cut the dough into long, 4 cm/1½ in wide strips. Place small heaps of filling every 4 cm/1½ in on half the strips. Brush the remaining strips with egg and press them over the ones with filling (leaving the brushed side downwards). Press around each heap to seal. Cut out even squares with the special wheel.

4. Boil ravioli, drain and serve with butter, grated Parmesan cheese and sage leaves.

ingredients

Pork and sage filling
> 315 g/10 oz ricotta cheese, drained
> 60 g/2 oz lean bacon, finely chopped
> 155 g/5 oz lean cooked pork, finely diced
> 1 teaspoon finely chopped fresh parsley
> ½ teaspoon finely chopped fresh sage
> 1 teaspoon grated fresh Parmesan cheese
> grated nutmeg
> freshly ground black pepper

homemade dough
> 3 cups/360g/12 oz plain flour
> 2 eggs
> 1 teaspoon salt
> 2 tablespoons safflower oil

Serves 4-5

tip from the chef

Sage is the ideal condiment for dense meats like pork.

seafood
lasagna

■ ■ □ | Cooking time: 60 minutes - Preparation time: 45 minutes

method

1. Preheat oven. Heat the oil in a large frying pan, add the leek and cook until tender. Stir in the tomatoes and tomato purée. Cook until mixture boils then simmer, uncovered, until sauce is slightly thickened. Stir in the prawn and fish pieces, cover and cook over low heat for about 5 minutes.

2. Cook the lasagna in a saucepan of boiling water until al dente. Place lasagna in a large bowl of cool water until ready to use.

3. Spoon one third of the sauce into the bottom of a 5 cm/2 in-deep casserole dish. Drain lasagna sheets and arrange a single layer over the seafood sauce. Spoon another third of the sauce over the lasagna, and top with another layer of lasagna.

4. Spread the remaining third of sauce over lasagna and top with mozzarella cheese. Bake at 180°C/350°F/Gas 4 for 40 minutes.

ingredients

> **2 tablespoons olive oil**
> **1 leek, white part only, finely chopped**
> **440 g/14 oz chopped canned tomatoes**
> **2 tablespoons tomato purée**
> **500 g/1 lb uncooked prawns, shelled and deveined, cut into small pieces**
> **250 g/8 oz boneless white fish fillets, cut into small pieces**
> **15 sheets spinach lasagna**
> **125 g/4 oz mozzarella cheese, thinly sliced**

....
Serves 4

tip from the chef

Lasagna is a hearty and plentiful dish, ideal for inviting guests or for large families.

tuna in piquant tomato sauce

■ □ □ | Cooking time: 35 minutes - Preparation time: 20 minutes

ingredients

> 1 tablespoon olive oil
> 4 fresh tuna cutlets
> 1 onion, chopped
> 2 cloves garlic, crushed
> 440 g/14 oz canned Italian peeled tomatoes, undrained and mashed
> 125 ml/4 fl oz tomato juice
> 2 tablespoons capers, chopped
> 4 anchovy fillets, chopped
> 1/2 teaspoon dried oregano
> freshly ground black pepper

method

1. Heat oil in a frying pan and cook tuna for 2-3 minutes each side. Transfer to an ovenproof dish and reserve juices.

2. To make sauce, cook onion and garlic in pan for 4-5 minutes or until tender. Add reserved pan juices, tomatoes, tomato juice, capers, anchovies and oregano. Season to taste with black pepper. Bring to the boil and pour over tuna. Cover and bake at 180°C/350°F/Gas 4 for 20-30 minutes, or until tuna flakes when tested.

....
Serves 4

tip from the chef

Tuna has an intensely flavored flesh that is high in fat. This sauce combines well with its taste and consistency.

sardine
fritters

a

■ ■ □ | Cooking time: 5 minutes - Preparation time: 35 minutes

method

1. Coat sardines in flour, dip in egg mixture, then coat with breadcrumbs.

2. To make minted chili butter, place butter, mint, spring onions, garlic, pepper and chili in a bowl (a) and mix well. Place butter on a piece of plastic food wrap (b) and roll into a log shape (c). Refrigerate until required (d).

3. Heat oil and one-third minted chili butter in a large frying pan and cook sardines for 1-2 minutes each side or until golden. Serve sardines topped with a slice of minted chili butter.

....
Serves 4

ingredients

> **12 fresh sardine filets**
> **4 tablespoons plain flour**
> **1 egg, blended with 2 tablespoons milk**
> **125 g/4 oz dried breadcrumbs**
> **oil for cooking**
> **125 g/4 oz butter, softened**
> **3 tablespoons finely chopped fresh mint**
> **2 spring onions, finely chopped**
> **1 clove garlic, crushed**
> **freshly ground black pepper**
> **1/4 teaspoon chopped red chili**

tip from the chef

Close to Naples the fish is eaten fried in olive oil with lots of garlic and herbs, accompanied by fragrant wines from the vineyards that are grown on those volcanic soils.

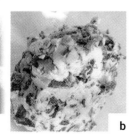

b

c

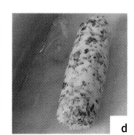

d

chicken with ricotta, rocket and peppers

a

■□□ | Cooking time: 30 minutes - Preparation time: 20 minutes

method

1. Preheat oven at 200°C/400°F/Gas 6. Combine ricotta, rocket, pine nuts, red pepper, ground pepper and salt in a small bowl (a) and mix together until smooth.
2. Place 1-2 tablespoons of ricotta mixture (b) under the skin of each chicken breast. Lightly grease a baking dish. Place the chicken breasts (c) in the dish, sprinkle with pepper and salt, place 1 teaspoon butter on each breast, pour stock around the chicken (d) and bake for 20-25 minutes.
3. Serve chicken with pan-juices and a rocket salad.

ingredients

> **200 g/7 oz fresh ricotta cheese**
> **1 cup rocket, roughly chopped**
> **¹/4 cup/45 g/1¹/2 oz pine nuts, toasted**
> **¹/2 red pepper, roasted and finely chopped**
> **freshly ground pepper and salt**
> **4 chicken breasts (200 g/7 oz each), with skin on**
> **1 tablespoon butter**
> **250 ml/8 fl oz chicken stock**

....
Serves 4

tip from the chef

These chicken rolls, stuffed with cottage cheese and pine nut kernels, deserve to be garnished with a good mix of green leaves.

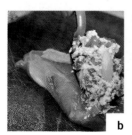
b

c

d

seared beef with
mushrooms and garlic

■□□ | Cooking time: 25 minutes - Preparation time: 35 minutes

method

1. Soak the porcini mushrooms in boiling water for 20 minutes. Drain and chop. Set aside.
2. Heat oil in a shallow pan and cook beef for a few minutes on each side. Remove from pan. Sauté the onion and the garlic for a few minutes, then add all of the mushrooms and cook over high heat until they are soft.
3. Add the wine and stock, bring to the boil, then simmer for 10 minutes. Remove from heat, add the parsley and season with salt and pepper.
4. Serve the beef with the mushrooms and sprinkle with extra chopped parsley.

....
Serves 6

ingredients

> 50 g/1 3/4 oz dried porcini mushrooms
> 60 ml/2 fl oz olive oil
> 1.2 kg/2 1/2 lb rump or fillet steak, cut into 6 steaks
> 1 brown onion, chopped
> 2 cloves garlic, crushed
> 350 g/12 oz shiitake/button mushrooms
> 60 ml/2 fl oz red wine
> 250 ml/9 fl oz brown stock
> 2 tablespoons parsley, chopped
> salt and pepper
> parsley, chopped (extra)

tip from the chef

Quick stir-fries, an Italian cuisine classic, go well with potatoes steamed and seasoned with olive oil.

pork
braised in milk

■ □ □ | Cooking time: 2¹/₄ hours - Preparation time: 10 minutes

method

1. Heat butter and oil in a large saucepan. When butter is foaming, add pork and brown on all sides.

2. Add milk, pepper to taste and bring to the boil. Reduce heat to low, cover and cook for 1¹/₂ 2 hours or until pork is cooked. Brush pork occasionally with milk during cooking.

3. At end of cooking time, milk should have coagulated and browned in bottom of pan. If this has not occurred remove lid and bring liquid to the boil, and boil until brown.

4. Remove meat from pan and set aside to cool slightly. Remove string from pork, cut into slices and arrange on a serving platter. Set aside to keep warm.

5. Remove any fat from pan, stir in water and bring to the boil, scraping residue from base of the pan. Strain and spoon pan juices over pork to serve.

ingredients

> **30 g/1 oz butter**
> **1 tablespoon vegetable oil**
> **1 kg/2 lb boneless loin pork, rolled and tied**
> **500 ml/16 fl oz milk**
> **freshly ground black pepper**
> **3 tablespoons warm water**

....
Serves 4

tip from the chef

This dish originates from Bologna and is often preceded by dishes with a Bolognese sauce. Pork cooked this way also goes well with artichokes.

garlic
veal steaks

■□□ | Cooking time: 15 minutes - Preparation time: 20 minutes

method

1. Heat half the oil in a nonstick frying pan over a low heat. Add garlic and cook, stirring until golden and soft. Remove garlic from pan and set aside.
2. Increase heat to high, add veal, lemon rind and thyme and cook veal for 1-1½ minutes each side. Remove steaks from pan, top with garlic, set aside and keep warm.
3. Heat remaining oil in frying pan over a high heat, add eggplant and stir-fry for 3 minutes. Add wine, tomatoes and basil and stir-fry for 3 minutes longer or until eggplant is tender. Season to taste with black pepper.
4. To serve, arrange veal, garlic and eggplant mixture on serving plates and serve immediately.

ingredients

> 1 tablespoon vegetable oil
> 6 cloves garlic
> 4 veal steaks or chops
> 2 teaspoons finely grated lemon rind
> 1 tablespoon chopped fresh thyme or 1 teaspoon dried thyme
> 1 eggplant, cut into matchsticks
> ¼ cup/60 ml/2 fl oz red wine
> 2 tomatoes, chopped
> 1 tablespoon chopped fresh basil
> freshly ground black pepper

....
Serves 4

tip from the chef

This dish is also delicious made with lamb steaks or chops instead of veal.

tiramisu

■□□ I Cooking time: 0 minutes - Preparation time: 20 minutes

ingredients

> **250 g/8 oz mascarpone**
> **1/2 cup/125 ml/4 fl oz cream (double)**
> **2 tablespoons brandy**
> **1/4 cup/60 g/2 oz sugar**
> **2 tablespoons instant coffee powder**
> **1 1/2 cups/375 ml/12 fl oz boiling water**
> **1 x 250 g/8 oz packet sponge fingers**
> **250 g/8 oz grated chocolate**

method

1. Place mascarpone, cream, brandy and sugar in a bowl (a), mix to combine and set aside. Dissolve coffee powder in boiling water and set aside.
2. Line the base of a 20 cm/8 in square dish with one-third of the sponge fingers. Sprinkle one-third of the coffee mixture (b) over sponge fingers, then top with one-third of the mascarpone mixture (c). Repeat layers finishing with a layer of mascarpone mixture, sprinkle with grated chocolate and chill for 15 minutes before serving.

....
Serves 4

tip from the chef

Mascarpone is a fresh cheese made from cream. It is available from delicatessens and some supermarkets. If unavailable, mix one part sour cream with three parts lightly whipped cream (double) and use in its place.

a

b

c

fig and mascarpone cake

■□□ | Cooking time: 5 minutes - Preparation time: 25 minutes

method

1. To make custard, place custard powder, sugar, milk, cream and vanilla essence in a saucepan and whisk until mixture is smooth. Cook over a low heat, stirring constantly, until custard thickens. Remove pan from heat and set aside to cool. Fold mascarpone into cooled custard and set aside.
2. Line a 23 cm/9 in springform tin with nonstick baking paper and line the base with half the sponge fingers. Sprinkle with half the marsala, top with half the sliced figs and half the custard. Repeat layers to use all ingredients. Cover with plastic food wrap and refrigerate for 4 hours or until cake has set.
3. Remove cake from tin. Decorate the top with extra figs.

ingredients
> **32 sponge fingers**
> **1/2 cup/125 ml/4 fl oz marsala**
> **6 fresh figs, sliced**
> **extra figs to decorate**

mascarpone custard
> **3 tablespoons custard powder**
> **2 tablespoons caster sugar**
> **1 cup/250 ml/8 fl oz milk**
> **1 cup/250 ml/8 fl oz cream (double)**
> **1 teaspoon vanilla essence**
> **375 g/12 oz mascarpone**

....
Makes a 23 cm/9 in round cake

tip from the chef
When figs are not in season, fresh strawberries make a suitable substitute for this elegant dessert.

choc-almond
biscotti

■□□ | Cooking time: 40 minutes - Preparation time: 20 minutes

ingredients

> **2 cups/250 g/8 oz flour**
> **3/4 cup/75 g/2 1/2 oz cocoa powder**
> **1 teaspoon bicarbonate of soda**
> **1 cup/250 g/8 oz sugar**
> **200 g/6 1/2 oz blanched almonds**
> **2 eggs**
> **1 egg yolk**

method

1. Sift together flour, cocoa powder and bicarbonate of soda into a bowl (a). Make a well in the center of the flour mixture, add sugar, almonds and eggs (b) and mix well to form a soft dough.

2. Turn dough onto a lightly floured surface and knead until smooth. Divide dough into four equal portions. Roll out each portion of dough (c) to make a strip that is 5 mm/1/4 in thick and 4 cm/1 1/2 in wide.

3. Place strips on a baking tray lined with nonstick baking paper. Brush with egg yolk and bake at 180°C/350°F/Gas 4 for 30 minutes or until lightly browned. Cut strips into 1 cm/1/2 in slices (d), return to baking tray and bake for 10 minutes longer or until dry.

....
Makes 35

tip from the chef

Biscotti may be partially dipped into melted chocolate for a two-toned effect. Before the chocolate sets completely, dip into toasted crushed almonds.

a

orange-pistachio
biscotti

■☐☐ I Cooking time: 40 minutes - Preparation time: 20 minutes

method

1. Sift together flour, sugar, baking powder and salt into a bowl.
2. Place eggs, egg whites, orange rind and vanilla essence in a separate bowl and whisk to combine.
3. Stir egg mixture and pistachio nuts into flour mixture and mix to make a smooth dough. Turn dough onto a lightly floured surface and divide into two equal portions. Roll each portion into a log with a diameter of 5 cm/2 in. Flatten logs slightly and place 10 cm/4 in apart on a nonstick baking tray. Bake at 180°C/350°F/Gas 4 for 30 minutes. Remove from oven and set aside to cool.
4. Reduce oven temperature to 150°C/300°F/Gas 2. Cut cooled logs into 1 cm/^{1}/$_2$ in thick slices, place on nonstick baking trays and bake for 10 minutes or until biscuits are crisp.

ingredients

> **2 cups/250 g/8 oz flour**
> **1 cup/250 g/8 oz sugar**
> **1 teaspoon baking powder**
> **pinch salt**
> **2 eggs**
> **2 egg whites**
> **1 tablespoon finely grated orange rind**
> **^{1}/$_2$ teaspoon vanilla essence**
> **75 g/2^1/$_2$ oz pistachios, shelled and toasted**

....
Makes 48

tip from the chef

Biscotti, other Italian food classic, accept all types of nuts: walnuts, almonds, hazelnuts and cashew nuts.

cassata
alla siciliana

■ ■ ■ | Cooking time: 15 minutes - Preparation time: 90 minutes

ingredients

> 4 eggs
> 1/2 cup/100 g/31/2 oz caster sugar
> 3/4 cup/90 g/3 oz self-raising flour, sifted
> 1/3 cup/90 ml/3 fl oz brandy

cassata filling

> 1/2 cup/125 g/4 oz sugar
> 2 tablespoons water
> 375 g/12 oz ricotta cheese
> 100 g/31/2 oz dark chocolate, finely chopped
> 60 g/2 oz glacé cherries, quartered
> 60 g/2 oz mixed peel, chopped
> 45 g/11/2 oz unsalted pistachios, chopped
> 1/2 cup/125 ml/4 fl oz cream (double), whipped

chocolate coating

> 315 g/10 oz dark chocolate
> 90 g/3 oz butter

method

1. Place eggs in a bowl and beat until light and fluffy. Gradually beat in caster sugar and continue beating until mixture is creamy. Fold in flour. Pour batter into a greased and lined 26 x 32 cm/101/2 x 123/4 in Swiss roll tin and bake at 180°C/350°F/Gas 4 for 10-12 minutes or until cooked when tested with a skewer. Turn onto a wire rack to cool.

2. To make filling, place sugar and water in a saucepan and cook over a low heat, stirring constantly, until sugar dissolves. Cool. Place ricotta cheese in a food processor or blender and process until smooth. Transfer to a bowl, add syrup, chocolate, cherries, mixed peel, pistachios and cream and mix to combine.

3. Line an 11 x 21 cm/41/2 x 81/2 in loaf tin with plastic food wrap. Cut cake into slices and sprinkle with brandy. Line base and sides of prepared tin with cake. Spoon filling into tin and top with a final layer of cake. Cover and freeze until solid.

3. To make coating, place chocolate and butter in a saucepan and cook, stirring, over a low heat until melted and mixture is well blended. Allow to cool slightly.

4. Turn frozen cassata onto a wire rack and cover with coating. Return to freezer until chocolate sets.

tip from the chef

Decorate this traditional Italian dessert with glacé fruits and serve as a special Easter, Christmas or wedding feast treat.

....
Serves 10

index